The Lover's Sigh

OrangeBooks Publication

1st Floor, Rajhans Arcade, Mall Road, Kohka, Bhilai, Chhattisgarh 490020
Website: **www.orangebooks.in**

First Edition, 2024

ISBN: 978-93-6554-556-2

THE LOVER'S SIGH

AN ANTHOLOGY OF ODES AND SONNETS

REX THOMAS

OrangeBooks Publication
www.orangebooks.in

This poem was written many years ago for my love, now my wife. I Dedicate **"The Lover's Sigh"** to her.

While I walked in a bush;
You came like a hush,
Leaves told many tales,
Stars appeared like hails,
Nocturne blue and my dreams,
Saturn's halo as it seems,
I stood and stared into heaven,
I heard your stories even,
Mighty my love, today I fly,
Caress my heart and I try,
Walk into the clouds nine,
Would I find a world of mine?
Tranquil wood nay talk,
But I'm not scared even to walk!
Alone I sleep –alone I weep,
You remain deep ...deep,
Into my eyes a dream lives,
A dream of your heart shines,

Here arrives a new kingdom of stars.

(This poem is, again, *her* choice as the beginner. It has no title)

“Love doesn’t need a praise, but acknowledgement”.

Poet

My word on TLS

Poetry is my soul. I wrote my first poem when I was barely 12 years old. But I never showed it to anyone, and I tore it after few years, as it was not a poem! Writing a poem is as easy or difficult as a swimmer floats on the water. He has to balance himself and has to use his legs technically. Same is with Poetry. It is a purposeful creation 'to enthuse and exult' in joy. Poetry is joy of language, beauty of vision, sight of soul and the best gift to your love! You can't be a poet without being a lover of any kind and the best poem is written when your heart is wrecked! TLS is simple and beautiful and my love is seen in my every poem. My love is kissed by my soul of words! My favourite among all is "SERE THE WORLD SANS YOU KEATS", as it's my tribute to a class lover and class thinker, John Keats. You shall find Shakespeare, John Milton, Robert Frost and an observer: that is, I, in TLS.

This book of anthology is not only for reading, but for feeling! A lover of the world and a lover of human; both can be in one person: hence THE LOVER'S SIGH.

Rex Thomas

Acknowledgement

John Keats is the only poet who inspired me with his fluent and effortless poetry. As I had my petite for poetry, I kept searching for Keats' complete work, but I was lost in the maze of duties and livelihood thence and I did not have a penny in hand to buy it from a bookstore. I kept penning poems and trashing it on the next day! Nevertheless, in one of my visits to a friend's home, I found a green, hard covered book, which was left unnoticed and filled with dust, which was nothing less than a miracle for me: The complete work of *John Keats. I read the book carefully and devoted my one month in order to understand it fully.*

I become a poet not because of John Keats, but I learned an ocean from his masterly written odes.

Poet

Contents

Oh, My Love Loneliness

"Oh! My love loneliness", mendicant mind anent,
Adjure in terse, amain heart; so wilt:
Alibi to breathe the perfect 'nose' without lament,
"Benthic"! Godly embraces of fondling bosom, shalt.
Rife, like marquetry quiet with denier feature;
Heard silent madrigal in ebbing passion!
Innocenc'd like a bairn, sweet like nectar;
Color'd like young roses; hair'd like golden furs in sun.
"Whilst chas'd the curvaceous waves: Loner lover,
Whilst scann'd the lonely moon: B'loved's warmth;
Whilst sung a nightingale, for nights lone, over –
Caressing wind;"vestal bride" with calm faith.
Accost in heart mine with 'sequins of love',
Bourn the hours, with sigh ever, lonely I saw.

***

The sonnet is written in praise of the poet's fondness for 'Loneliness'. His desire for being alone and considers the loneliness is not boring, but his *beloved. It's calm and beautiful.*

Toddler's Dream Never Comes True

Winds do damn my *castle of dreams*,
Plough others with blessings of bliss screams;
As "joy gain"; precarious; lords earn still cosy,
Deepen fever mine true; the dreams be,
Dry fields mine, yet zoom around honey bee!
Nor sow, nor crop; birds migrate,
Spare everybody, immers'd half my legs under rate.

Tax'd being mine, vain enough by,
Wax'd feelings mine, hopes close to die!
Travel lot me, unfluke most, no tavern –
I do see, in the path were along to govern.
Mute or deaf me not, sough or puff me not,
Meticulous at times; tune heart mine; pity clarinet.
Stake what 'being mine' puffed in string –
Of queries, stretch my arms at the helpless brink.

Wait for long, me lone traveller at –

Crumbl'd ambitions, dimpl'd dreams, yet –

Chang'd inns of support nethermost

Chang'd ski's blue to grey,remain lost –

Paradise for no good, by virtue to any may;

"Empty palms mine, worth my future nay".

Slog's fragile, sleeps water fram'd, mishaps

Once nor twice, in my vacuum sphere, perhaps!

Heart mine is an *antique* in value least,

Bring virtue once n'ver, but ever by death best;

N'ver sure as best in birth and best in death; ever one:

"Jesus" the lord thou ,thou, thou alone !

I dreamt of mounts and ponds, valley'n paddy;

N'ver bloom, but bleak; hear the murmur cry, nor melody!

"May this be cuss worst to the toddler,

May this be, ever dream to fly high, 'very toddler."

***

The poet is wailing on his unsuccessful attempts. He is failing repeatedly, he is far behind his achievements despite his best efforts. Neglect, contempt and rejection. He considers him a child and his dreams are getting perished.

Sere The World Sans You Keats

B'hest the moon, garland'd with golden rhyme
Recherche impromptu versus with lancet pen;
Unleash'd myths of 'Victorian epoch': Phonetic hymn;
Tour de force odyssey'd in pelagic poesy when-
"Young as seven, older with twenty too":
"How old are you, ocean with unseen views?"
Akin thee 'John' how tender! Larks coo-
B'side, stood he unsow'd field, sparse pelf: tease!
Indit'd with inundating fragrance of gourds:
Writ for 'Lamia, The Eve of St.Agnes and Endymion',
Like 'Bright Stars' 'On the sea' and many odes:
'To Psyche' to 'Autumn' and 'Gracian Urn'.
Indolent physique turn all about to postern,
Ordain'd God, the weekend, *yet spring* for you 'John'!

***

A Word About The Sonnet:

This is the toughest sonnet I ever countered with, for its main character John Keats. It is not possible by any poet to bring his entire glory in 14 lines. This is however, I confess, not a perfect 'light on Keats'. Poet is lamenting on the untimely demise of John, 'he was young as seven, but twenty years more' he lived! Therefore, he left the world at a young age, the age of actual spring of life span of a human, so he will remain fresh forever.

And, unless you have read Keats' poems, it would be impossible to comprehend this sonnet.

Poet

Genius

Cool thy head in rain when,

Roar the thunder above;

Dine at peace when burn,

The whole earth, below!

(Satire)

Lama

I

Unmow'd roughs and heal the unfed,
Post-haste limbs, neat mop'd head, nor gear'd;
Clad well part black hate to kiss foot-
So neck; God-son acumen eyes hot,
Yellow fac'd monk, unshoddy heart –
Like wild buff's horn , whispers to air ,
All a Lama, who born in flames, lives apart –
Mesh'd lairs of undrain'd dirt;
Unrav'd monk, people debunk and un-debonair.

Lama's lores read, perceiv'd past,
Every present is mother'd in the past;
Laddie the monk like youthsome bloom,
Solace the grace of words like chill'd dew –
Fiery heart fear not, hear people near less gloom,
Least he in throng's encore yet, adieu –
Autumn of smiling stray blossoms;

Di-do the people, who ply without bosoms,
Diadems of truth: demon's hymns!

Where do occupy the richless Lama in –
The castl's of dinky metaphors, may abhor,
His preaches are burn'd out gold, rul'd out the inn-
Mates; Lama without aroma sunk unadore.
Chivalrous castes offer'd cactus bed;
Tow-path'd until, another winter-berry tales-
Be found, wisp of wisteries and smile dead!
Many miles to go, seen live images of human wails,
Left torsos untow'd, thaw hopes and afraid.

Baffl'd ambitions, strife how more be?
May-fly desir's; Lama the untrac'd glory:
Unlit lamp, unrisen sun, all may not vary;
Cach'd the relique of feelings not to be –
Any evil's comfort 'merchandise him to silence'!
Waters flown and stories well- read least once,
For Lamas young to draw new light;
Forsake and forgive to the mother decades.

II

Fervent truths of reality, no medley reverent;
‘Genie’ may visible be in you, at home and nation,
Scaffolds are left for those scarce ‘it’;
Lama, the scorn yesters: bemourn emotion –
Morrow sure; grandchild decades,
Fend themselves in sin of mothers.
Break the air of silent crim’s,
And to be torn the barbarous texts;
Cease the massage to the living demons.

Lama taught and fed, mundane fool’d,
Mug both vice and wise here; left aroma,
None stood for, occupied he in scaffold un-rivall’d.
Mark’d as a ‘true apostle’, chain’d Lama;
Few the unswindl’d desist in mute cries,
Blind’d him with lack-lustre clothes;
Sunk the cries in the *otiose encore* of ‘lingeries’.
Disguis’d Lama liv’d and died; undermin’d,
Every human is evil unless God train’d!

III

Shalt this proem for the hang man?

Under born annums may all set to candescent;

Gun powders and cannons spur through, when –

Lingo of hatred, vamp of war, do foment,

Castes to castes, zone to zone, blood to blood!

Smooch the snack of 'glued dust' –

Worried Lama stood in rock and tranquil 'glad',

Liquidate the helmsman to clay and heist –

Cheers, tears of tired Lama; none to applaud!

***

Summary: Lama is the epitome of truth and innocence who has taken every hardship on his shoulder with a smile on his face in order to save the world from all kinds of wars either it is caste, community of language, the world would be in ruins unless it is ceased. But the world has petrified him, his fight against the bad in his own way- which somehow resembles the pain suffered by Jesus Christ. Lama is a saviour.

Souls Never Die

Groovin' calls of forest heads,
Timorous the lives silent under leaf beds!
Grindin' 'small heart' in the timpani'd air-
Tend my paws to blot my maid's tear.

Fiddler a, somewhere, burgeon'd sad;
D'part souls of the mate: fain notes,
Playin' lightly in broken rods!
Meddling no one, but seldom tears shed.

'Souls ne'er die', but sources,
If soul itself the innate source, leases-
'Vain' or may 'gain': joy or annoy,
Blame whom he, in not bouy even scrawny.

'Livin' memoriam brings back,
The souls of 'dears'; one hath it once –

Least in the seasons any may lack-

Lustre and grimace, shall name sad'est he'vens?

Radiant blossoms sad unless –

Reach humming purl of romeo beetl's;

May a heaven of souls, nature's bless,

Show'd all cri's and lolls lov'ly kettl's.

***

Memories of a great act, which had the human self is imprinted or inherited, irrespective of love or anger or loss, you may not be able to forget it, the soul of the loved act or thing or person may be around you as the poet says… 'soul never dies…'!

"A Smile Is A Symbol Of What You Are"

Ode To Darkness

I

Fate deem'd row days on earth,
Perdurable sun perdite till eve;
My ode is ugly indeed, for dark worth;
'Lurable darkling' sea's and den's have-
'Painter brush'; ever forte scripts;
Abstract but nude the 'maid' for –ever-more.
All darken'd darlings: potable wines,
Albeit may n'ver acclaim'd sure;
Loyal bride she mine, ever not Keats' glory;
Of blemish and snag of scorn!
Faithful belov'd thee in my heart sad prone;
When fiddl's sorrow, no bright in need,
No squeals wriggle in the lead!

II

Transit the sphere looks sick sick widow;
Unless night drunk 'black wine' dope!
All the fair ladies squirm sashay flirt vow,

Nor she a jasmine cradle in the night's lap.

The silent reach of bright smiles of sun,

Great the nymphs of dumb night;

Mimic the people in predecessor's cult;

Spright in fair, everywhere for no damn!

Odes well accolade pretty, fairy days,

Shamble the sad bride of darkness;

Sham! Not night, but light: vive guys.

No verse in prodigy for the long calls, cloudless,

Amok'd the perch'd gestures in the night – rains;

Rattl'd the darkness, dwellings and mansions.

III

Darkling the host courteous when heaven blink,

Wallow, the lives in debt, the lovers' sigh;

Waive all squawks and praise the hunk;

Nepenthe the night; undo everything and lie,

Till the shining quest wakes, muffle all sins.

Wanton the light when warble fills;

Peer the creatures in blinks with jeer.

Unslept the 'nightingale' flew in vigour,

Erratic 'her' caravan with pule loaded-

Lyrics, wails to the night-hood;
Incinerate her anguish in the broad bosom-
Of the "moll of hell", but my "comfort dom"!
"Rational thine fair days may and pry –
Not darkling; national none shadowed sundry!"

IV

Fiesta, every glorifi'd in darkling crackers;
Sultry the heart: the toil'd folks,
Nights the best ope the eas'd lockers –
Of sigh'd nap, glory to darkling flicks.
Hay-wire the birds, hamlet when in shades;
Eyes, the fiancé of pulchritude, self be dark-
Grapes; hearken my plea for heaven sakes,
"Haws hung in the field, hay-rick seen, sung lark-
Shackle all sad, the hay-man's gay too dark,
Dark, dark the mud for apples sweet;
Slays them the 'people-in-lights', spare our mirk."
Romancing the 'dark ink' on rags, very treat –
For poets, like primitive wines, may –
Rhyme Odes in notes unleash'd at bay.

***

Explanation: I believe, it is at times difficult to convey the pain directly to another person by mouth, but to a true reader it is quite easy. The Ode begins with the perception of people on the dark of a day (night time) then it slowly moves to the critical part and to the glory of darkness. The poet praises darkness, as he can't see anyone even not he himself…, but his pain is 'self struck'. He enjoys the stars in the night, the nightingales' playful safari in night. He is sad for many reasons and he considers the darkness his bride…!

If Thou Be...

If thou be a flower borne vineyard:
I canst have a placid mood to care long.

If thou be a stream heaving noisy flow:
I canst have a bath in splendour water blow.

If thou be a dream in unforeseen hours:
I canst come with you in all moments.

If thou be a baby, for the mom, sweetest:
I canst kindle and cradle loll with merry.

If thou bea lily odours best:
I canst smellst thou, nose to ankle, full.

If thee be a sea, long-wide –blue-deep:
I may be the voyager along your waves.

If thee be a castle of pearl best:
Be me the happiest king in heart thine.

If you be a queen anywhere under sky:
Oh, sure my heart will embellish thou cleave.

If you be the smooth, nice sands on banks:
I'll roll around, mad, till die thee for!

If you be the nicest shades of Angelo or Vinci:
Put thou billion times in colours, on walls of love.

If thou be a star in night late sky:
Will I drop the wink, wish last, ere death?

If thou be a breeze, enough me to crazy be:
I'll open the lanes of love thatched hut, with may full.

If thou be an angel of 'God', I believe:
May I be the message, bear thee thus me everywhere.

If thou be a fine clear ink:

I'll write an Ode in love, for love, endless.

If thou be the clay best and bright:

Mould I'll belle in you, with you, shines stun!

If thou be the sweetest, neatest honey:

I'll be the beetle black, vigour and gentle.

If thou be the symphony to cool ears:

Compose, I'll, the melody n'ver heard, the best.

If thou be a vision mine:

Thou I see in every sight, feel and pretty.

If thou be the love pure, named many:

'Choose thou me, the lover best, my hum nice.

(This is a dream of the poet about his 'imagination' of 'how his ideal beloved should be. So he finds everything in the world is a form of love.)

"Everyone Is an Idiot, Until Awake."

Snowfall In Christmas

I

Purgatorial weigh'd sphere chide;
Reprieve rock'd air whose abode?
Landslide wound'd; morgue ic'd valley,
Green in cool opulence, croon the trolley.
'Snowfall beauteous', rout and frost,
Arson'd innocents down too crude-
Sheer some huts and lamp'd in rust;
'Snowfall in Christmas', no horse rode!

II

Trebl'd owls, w'en two winds meet;
Scamp rose –marys in hot cabinet,
Orific'd mouths in wonder, owls and gnats,
Winds pass'd in shame, 'unheld candl's '-
On Christmas ever since frost begins!
Myrtle, yet green and skip to grow, awaits,
Day frost or hot, crisps short and ic'd,
Svelte pats of colour'd wind short pac'd.

III

Rookie the winds, snowfalls too be;
Lovers at station untrace'd, pain treat'd
"How shall cry when seas dry, skies dash'd ,
Boulders walk and mounts speak chubby"?
Preen the snow like a puck's dreams!
Puissance like gritty teddy bear, wind roams,
Drunk sumac pulp; wind rattl'd , sun plump;
As old Greek castles, hearts unlit dump.

IV

Warren universe, stars hide,
Solitaires amber tread and cri'd,
Vied them once in, puddle, colour and chaste!
On this Christmas, but winds in no haste,
First the fiesta to be, snowfall hinder,
N'ver them in unison, to share the love seem,
Deem how much in dreams, whims lover!
Snowfalls undeem'd shalt rock lovely hum.

V

Mayhem intricate inside hearts',
Christmas love shall be oracl'd,
Ornary winds wander'd, unhear'd shouts,

Anacondas and celestial reptiles heaved –
In hearts once lov'd and wind flown!
Frost the hearts like oolite hard;
"Rap the Christmas up ere jarr'd,
Trap the hearts under snow fallen."

VI

Epistles of love: hemlock for life;
Till death; some bitter, some sweeter,
Beckon! Cease praising frost reef,
Till hearts cure, wind blows later,
Christmas too be, winter miracles,
"Fiddle the hearts of innocent lovers,
For infidel frost and snowfalls torrid,
Hugs of sweet rays run-off and taunt'd."

VII

Rut seemst neither rip soon;
N'ver stroll'd mermaid hearts-
In heaps of words like fugitive moon,
Bou –doirs of estrang'd beloveds –
Unglare,even if jewell'd walls any,
Frost hearts, snowfall rock'd, worri'd,

"Christmas under the pines of rainy-

Ice balls,true the lover: unlit candles, not cri'd."

***

(The poet is wailing on the heavy snowfall which caused hundreds homeless, died and still suffering while others are lavishly enjoying Christmas! How will the lover get his beloved in the frost all around to tell… 'His love for her and it is his life'. Read the pain of the poet …stanza 3, lines 3 and 4.)

"A Lover Needs No Eyes To
Love."

Ode To Dream

I

B'like a liege b'loved when morose –
Silken heart with soothe embrace,
Ethereal lots, 'the nymph of drowse';
In liaison with my soul: Zinging grace.
Wisp of smiles sweeten hearts lovelorn,
'She 'everyone's whim, quip in silence;
'Deep kiss'd lips' of dream: the sassy boon;
'Dish'd neat me', the lass with all essence!

II

Like a wahine on the waves,
Whiz at times 'reticent',whet stiff asleep;
With mermaid loof both halves,
Wile the willowy belle in every step.
Revel my nights with balsam flowers,
Wily,left brisk hither–to suspense,

"Reigning the brides all to the dream lovers:
Folly the charm of dream, hail and incense!"

III

I travell'd in the dream offere'd –
Shore; in colours of 'haste and frills',
With smiles like 'Madeline bride'!
"Whom count'd huts lit, all heaven fills,
None wound'd, infidel fiancée mine, by!"
All dreams sought not the chaos booby,
When 'Porphyro' shed blood in all rile,
All meant scant nor: For bride's wile!

IV

Strode the rook weening brain:
'Lyres and pipes sung by seraphims',
Glow'd loggia like a sun'd rain,
Live long bountiful locus …, saucy hums,
For me and for you, may cynic me;
Shalt more nor, thee dream the *lovely wench!*
"Prithee! I wish, I own my love along roamin' –
Sand dunes, fell'd spirited wings with all punch!

V

D'monic some dream: D'moisell apparition,
Haze dawn and dusk in pantaloon'd sulk,
Like a 'horrorful epic' with devil's mission;

Lieu of glow worms, hawks with rack;
"Sieg'd rally of life with benison'd maid,
Little with any 'pants or pansy', some may void!"

VI

Scum muslin she wore and addle-
Banshee! Bustling nightmares in ebony woods;
Envoy'd eagles, ossuaries delv'd and huddle-
Panopli'd witches, purlieu 'fear gods'!
"Scull'd brooks with serpentine gyre,
Null'd dreams, all nor fair maids,etching fear."

VII

"Ave –Maria", none sung but view,
Misty Alps seem'd newly dress'd;
Silently niggle, the pined brides with dew;
Silver lei, and green velvet hush'd.
"Easel's envy, these earthly brides; how dandy,
Unshow'd angels heave's contrite;
No matter, thee wed dream! Dream so handy",
B'little the 'crimson cheeks' far and bright.

VIII

Does what he search, silent sun?

Espi'd the foggy vale, Oh, blissful reality;

Ever 'laddie' the sun, so old no burn!

Ever dream I, hunk of lasting fidelity,

"Sheer the soulless hag of fallacy –

Sun and Alps true; me my soul true;

Slam'd no 'friary surf' in the whole sea,

Luffing psyche, panes shut nix dream grew!

IX

Of siblings loveth, reveri'd tender limbs-

Aghast 'laughing world',launder all sins!

"Thy remember St.Agnes' mercy, no dream numbs."

Sane no lover: Insane the writ lines,

All winds no hint, seeketh frantic pain;

Odd dreams, hoard'd mine thought,

"Oh,love…shalt my realm ne'er reign:

Nonce world; no row, no foe and haught?"

***

"ODE TO DREAM": Is a difficult Ode which I wrote, but I enjoyed writing it. I start loving the dreams, which became true, never became true, some are real fallacy.

Every kind of dream is alive in this ode. At some point I felt whether I am a fool to love ‘dream’ too. When your dream becomes love, your love becomes a dream for others.

“A dream should not be your nightmare, but the day fare!”

L.O.V.E

Least clouds, skies blue,

Odour fresh every morn and ev',

Virtue, sharing, hearts two;

Endless wide sea flames marvel.

(In this poetic pinch, each line begins with a letter of the word LOVE in the ascending order, but ends each line in the reverse order EVOL)

Cease Whom My Cry?

Harbinger's yell not his will, unwick'd lamp;
Wreck'd b'fore ever liv'd, grey'd heart and lump,
Stingy his plunder'd verve life;
May ne'er embank any "choir" in vertiginous "half"!
In du-bio, my brother, in colour of 'blooms',
Litter'd in the armor'd pot of b'trayals!
Poppy-cock this life be; granted in vista;
Twitters 'very averse in, ails and he in 'siesta'.
Fleck'd my heart with verdant meadows,
Hopes all aches and burns sans, near 'equator';
Gloss me like veneer, whenever in shadows-
Vertex'd sorrows and laments; reason in my prayer!
'Bru-tum ful-men', he mayn't veer'd through;
'Cease whom my cry', he my brother though!

(This sonnet was written on my brother whom with I lived my eleven long years. He fell ill once and lost his body weight drastically and the ailment continued for long and gradually I thought I would lose him. The fear made me write the sonnet as a prayer. I was severely acknowledging his pain)

"Don't Learn How To Love, Feel When You Love."

Lacunae At Fifty

Avert none can the dirt on
Peasant’s bare foot,
Slow down the pace b’fore them reach
Ill thatch’d hut;
A day went by, near the tranquil
wall of teeth’d poverty.
Flow down from the stale eyes,
but no ears to hear the sky!

Glori’d whom? Bless’d whom?After
years fifty!
Merri’d the lords and ladies; fly less
on earth, more in lofty,
Mention the tension of screaming
Down trodden's, whom
Made your lord to govern: the bloody
human worm!

Wane lantern in sky, fair
enough till morn' –
W'ere the folk lay head down under
the blazing sun;
Me too; rest b'neath host-dry
trees of summer;
Shall anyone hope more shade under
leafless trees slimmer!

In the realm of liberty, we dream of
Cast'less territory,
Vernacular differs nei'bour to
nei'bour, class too dreary;
Bounds more', fail the rulers past;
sounds very brutal!
Nor in heaven you worth, w'en vulture
liv's in will fatal!

Neither you nor I, freed apart, as long
tyrrant' sceptor mov's;
Along with 'patriotic saints' of Indian
soil blames the conny cronies!

Poor we, idiot we; be in unison: sarcasm
like; ghost … grows;
Lay back in hovels; less re'd or ink'd,
put in abrupt.

Years fifty gone in haste; left many
in waste,
Hears lofty the terms and no token for
Freed least;
No more milk teeth left in us; proud
little we,
Unless be fell'd the golden teeth and the
Silver means of the attorney!

***

It revolves around the 'tale of two countries: India and Pakistan. Both countries are arch rivals, long years of conflicts, conciliations and talks are of no benefit till date. Fifty three years of discussions could not help each other. [*This poem was written twenty seven years ago, hence it was used 'fifty years'. Today, after seventy seven years too, both countries remain hostile each other. I want to know 'who will accept who is at fault, my answer is – 'both'!*]

PS: Both countries want peace, both countries have a lot in common, both countries have its number of kith and kin living without seeing one another for decades, even their grandparents or parents end their lives without seeing their children! Is it the way to solve the dispute? When the possibility of 'war and peace' is equal, it is wise to choose the latter. But, a third element is disturbing the peace process between these two nations!

"One of the most solvent places I ever have seen, THE GOLDEN TEMPLE, Amritsar, Punjab (India). *A poet like me can write endless poems while seeing it in the moonlit night. An inspiring momento..."*

A Tribute

A true lover must be a good dreamer and he makes his every dream true, hence he becomes inspiration to others. It is recommended by the instincts of a lover to find love in every beautiful thing! And beauty remains unchanged ever after generations. The finest writers always found everything beautiful, which doesn't hurt, pain or pollute.

"...a thing of beauty is a joy forever" (John Keats)

Poet

"Is beautiful duty or dutiful beauty preferred by you?
The former will divide and the latter will reside."

Lone Shone Moon

Tight the fleet of ashed shades,
Vales and valoured heads mute and stood,
Momentous abduction heralded here lores,
Gales so fooled, 'held high spirits' head:
Selfless groom hides 'tween breasts –
Broaden revolves relentless, silent;
Serene the night, my bride not in jewels,
Banished light even, heaven may ignorant,
"Face-off my new moon bride from ashes dark,
Glazes high of gold on embers red and spark."

Kinder my heart then, tender the night;
Pass a moment in lanky shades,
Kissed *unlanguidly on her full* right;
Sleighing out in golden grin amids',
Open eyed bio-statues on earth;
Arrested feelings in inmates dashed.
Errand my bride; bright unbetrayed love for both,

Lead us in true lamp pale, yet well saved;
“True, true wives might spright in tight bowel,
Find her lambs merried, vast,vast her love to reveal.”

She hates when clouds stir and errant;
Imperial her vigour and charm and earnest,
Ever paid she in kind and love so pregnant;
No wind may pamper, neither greenest;
Golden *the mentor wrought penny may cost,*
Ring changeling in the dark castle, brought he;
Saw sure for moments few; repelled both in haste,
Loved them bare in the home of dark lea.
Tinted swart the realm under,
Like coalside dust spread asunder.

Sung very loud in the green cloudy,
Penchant peacock with heart full shy:
Without penance they danced; peeved the moon,
Why odours those bulbs foot hills faraway –
Might be confession late night today.
Cirrus shined after cuddle; lie –
Onus adieu, years to meet; till lone.

Ceased opera set to the roost and grey;
“Rare so meet love so hard and heard,
Numbed music in the garden of sad.”

Spring day sadness: full moon madness,
Eternal the shameless lassie spares not,
Earth so vast, clothe the ‘bridal dress’,
Lover ‘he’ unique forebear virgin’s knot;
Kneel we obliged for her lantern undoused,
Adieued promos at hour midnight-
Freak endorsed reality, I beau, loved;
Tantrums antique moon’s, ever so bright;
Lulled clouds wield around and cried,
Nulled denizen’s sorrow after full lit bride.

Recent the snow, odour mud ascents,
Better nor less to felicitate the moon’s odes;
“All odes prey virgin houri, none widow’s glory,
Artisan best he poet; unless nether world worships.”
Reeds of moon’s occult oboe; she loves,
With occasional vacations once and sorry;
Little inveigh her learned jest,

Unscrolled tales many, same sad, my lady love;
"Ever nil victor lover any, moon so high behest,
To own or to bestow; trust she ever and now."

Less or more human life a moon likely,
Crescent, half and full; undeemed kinds,
Child, youth and rest; ungalored smile,
Unseen her lofty tantrums drowsy humans,
Seas garlanded with frenzied tides;
Beseemed loving pet speechless wags tail in loyalty;
Still was the woo as greenhill mounts,
'Will'with berserking love, all the same, novelty.
Shamed peacocks stood in amaze, ugly his legs,
Moon's tantrums eternal: fractional waves sea's.

***

Unwinged birds filled to flee past;
Felled in the doldrums of skies denounced,
The spirits vitrious moaned, but rest –
The vanishing vampires in disguised –
Wardrobes of 'kept' intrigues may grim;
"Never knot any groom without riot scrapped,
And the greys may renown with dreams trim!"

Bred no saints on costumes well draped,

Breed all kinds of monsters in the wall,

‘Fair this earth and moon if love we all spell.’

***

Poesy this may best by soul mine,

Sooth my beloved’s artful eyes shine,

Every night with unfeelable touch,

Yet sulken the silky bride all her march.

Shut this eve of love forth, promises kept;

Waking the jasmine bulbs lazy, still rapt.

Soar my heart onto the heaven of ‘moon so lone’;

My love she ever in unblameful shy;

Dame the broke walls and tamed my love soon,

“Rhyme this psalm beneath the boon so high.”

***

[A note on one night of lunar eclipse. I wrote this poem at one go in the same night. A blissful night and moonlit sky]

"Shades Are Not Beautiful, But Trees Are."

Ode To Youth

Unripen'd the fruits hung, sway'd in the wind loony;
Staid the flesh, lucent rivulet of thoughts,
Hedonistic 'Luncheon' in fad with honey,
The 'mist' of adolescence: fake 'orb' of hosts!
The 'island of lust' and leviathan'd luxury,
Mad madrigals in the 'woods of oaks' so temptress;
I sit, sinew'd bard, found blooms dry,
Bright, bright no dark, 'Oh youthful empress'!
"N'ver, n'ver I love to skip the sandal dense,
Fragrance forever, fright the eve of ignorance!"
Like 'a day or a night': clay'd wares,
Perish'd everyone's; furtive islands;
"Oh, youth, thou be ever for a bard like I,
Whether or not an inclement supper, nor fond by!"

***

The sonnet depicts the most pleasant phase of life*: the youth. .... "N'ver, n'ver I love to skip the sandal dense,*

Fragrance for ever, fright the eve of ignorance!"

John Keats inspired me to write this sonnet. It is simple and direct. The poet seldom likes to grow older as he loves his youth. Everyone enters once and it is submerged as a temporary island.

"A Poet Dies Many Times, But Never Gets Buried."

Dieu Vous Garde Mother

Enmoss'd figures over gales,
Rust and drudgery heart bails,
Enmass'd dreams rivall'd my just;
'Murky unmush'd realms of beast.'
Says heart in ruesome self unfair,
Gales blown in rhyme, bids in fire.

Fare well past, marvel tire,
Temples loiter'd mother's mine often;
Unbridl'd her love in ill or cure,
Yearn this child, so long, stiffen;
Mom she compassionate like,
Piano old'n gentle; I so bleak.

Mother she pois'd and a lake-
Of love, blearly she fed me;
"Thou my mom, flood me proud,
All forest towers blithe in rain, ye look."

Train'd me unfathom'd ruth,
Rustic my mother no laurel, is truth.

Comb'd hair, when ag'd runt,
Car'd me like her eye;
Canst nor fetch 'gales pass'd hunt',
Enisle heart in deathless ennui.
"May be skies or be waters,
May be earth or be all what mother's."

Evergreen meadows little graz'd cows,
Sooth, when rains abstain, under;
More alike mother mine now yonder;
Portiere hung across to-morrows.
Beseech my heart mom, behest –
'Gales' ripen'd, lives in bracket.

Hot eyes mine with tears borne,
Root of all unmeasur'd sorrows;
Vary thee not mother, nor shown:
Swore I to serve, but narrows-

Nor more larky lad me, mother's gloom;
'No cradle left, gales but with zoom'.

Cook'd rice and flavour'd meals;
Kiddish mud and undevour'd zeals.
Vocated me still not, yet seek,
Scourge ye mayn't, ye weak!
For hands mine not lent w'en ye ache,
'Severe let not Lord, her, at the peak.'

Pardon this child unserv'd,
N'ver me choose crab apples for thee,
Fledgling me shalt; now brav'd,
Sans 'gales' air may sad, world so ugly;
"Best ever mothers, kids shall rest,
Gales or storms fails ere mother's breasts."

***

I still and ever cry for not able to be by my mother's side. She is an unmatchable fragrance in my life. I want to see my mother every day. Perhaps at her old age she needs me the most, I need her the most!

No one is fortunate, if his mother is not around, don't leave her alone, …love her, ...live her! My intense pain is visible in the poem.

"If you can see me, then why I need my eyes, and if you can't feel me, then why I need a life?"

Aggrieved Hearts.

Ring the harness in ‘heaven’ assent;
Unwrap the graves in ‘eve’ nascent,
Rebuild the lobbies to there, sledge dark clouds,
“Had been the clouds unclean, home mine; alas!
Rampage eve without gaze fair ever ere;
Savage the wind, nod the stouts back and fore.

Scourge my heart in entangl’d melancholy;
Put boulders big on way mine to heaven.
Spirits vice riot my path in every eve unholy,
Wander hearth on earth ravenous human,
Candour the waves, course eve; might –
To rectify true com-passionate love bright.

Victor thee, I’m a factor in human many,
Hope neither me lash’d, for honest matrimony,
“Desert those love, who be coward to knight,
Dessert those another with trust, steward and might.”

Flower fell’d driven none goof, all proof;
But graced divine those by the pontiff roof!

Blithe some cuss’d, right be bless’d death!
Least worth emerald until eyed, rank’d in light;
My heart so deepest in least; unknown myth,
Throw your oars when current favour under moonlight;
Shed the clouds of eve, be wed the eve sun red;
Thy cheeks, shalt me never in hatred.

Countless ‘eves’ past and blowing present;
Freed the ghost of ‘dissent’ in hearts may relent –
Crusade heaven-wise; revise stories untold,
“A poet shalt lay on spear-bed, sure hold,
Romantic inkstand and set-in endless elegies!
Best the rest say, hect his feather like burning effigies.”

Weakest my days, when brings peakest pain every ‘eve’,
Idiot poets repair it with scant scent poetry!
Long, long the disguis’d love profound which lave,
Nights, dawns and days in dispens’d joy; yet try,

Fir-tree X'mas in snow and pit-hole candles,
All's the rhyme when one loves: when belov'd fondles.

'Hearts or the love remain little after bid'
Those notes carved for the love impart'd shalt be rigid.
How immortal those lines with melody'n melancholy;
As 'Gracian Urns', with sculptur'd sermons;
Divine the love refin'd in heaven, its no folly,
Larger be the 'sum' when human departure costs!

'Eves' in dark and 'nights' in lights: ruthless, unfair;
Man without *heart and heart nor love:* Godless heaven!
Regardless my fear be, every human once or more.
Still thee in dozless flames of lantern;
"Longest, longest wail frill in borest, borest eve falls,
In sadd'st, sadd'st hell of earthly *angels."*

Unravish'd, tranquil tales may be raped;
The sweeter melodies thou heard once;
"Esquisite charm of gods and goddesses,
When in requisite verduring passion burns."

Let the unheard melodies be scrapp'd,
If bitter thine melodies heard and trapp'd.

Golden poesy 'on thee' written,
Green marshy the opiate paddy blooms;
All over radiate, oblivious eyes mine,
Free the idle autumn, silent the near willows.
Repertoire begins toads, crows and cranes;
Repent of the early night, stood me in silence.

Unprecedent'd the altering climax,
Frost head'd shepherd lives, dies son at six!
Unchang'd the opaque human memories,
Varied in stature and fracture; nor nice,
'Eve': *dreary my desert land of courtesy;*
Truesome memoir view'd, vantage nil mercy.

The dissent consensus rendezvous in pale unwild eve,
Set the dessert in chamber, where admirals did rest;
Faery's hue not heard: nor I in love;
Lost most 'heaven', host the 'eve' I hate;

Neither 'she' nor 'me' in quiet, seemst nor be;

More aggriev'd hearts ours ever be!

***

It's the frustration of the suffered commoner, where he lives, all those things which make him sad and idle. He doesn't find it an ideal time to blossom love. He is worried about the "dreariness of the land he lives", but most of the citizens are not concerned even. Aggrieved hearts!

"Eternal Things Can Never Be Over Done!"

Any More Summer Rains

Mind so wind sure-
Wind so free,
Dart merry, if mere –
A life to be.

Saints shall preach –
Nor breach;
Among us and treach-
In time fetch.

Mother feeds the child-
It cries if;
Shivering breeds mild-
Never tries of.

Fake hoardings in hearts-
Seek coins gold;

Lake so deep, but looks –
May never hold.

Some shall feed doves –
Fail to feed home!
Waste the grains –
Bins even gloom!

I scale even my days –
Odd occur many;
Why heal not the dogs,
Without any penny?

Poets I've seen many; nor-
Like I any;
Browning, Hardy, Keats and Mare –
In heart, so funny.

Hard a hut to be burn' -
Lads gay -out;
Unti'd gears laid in –
Lays evening note.

May please someone me by –
Everyone n'ver;
Shall truth their hautbouy-
Play it for ever.

Jump into the famine sea –
Dumps on board,
Cry very loud heart be –
Within mounts broad.

Sun at midnight sought –
None, but fun.
Shone the *shameless moon*, but –
Even stars not seen.

Asunders of clouds let –
Poor down,
Doors are shut, huts repent –
In water flown.

Bloom'd roses and jasmine, dri'd –
Both in summer.

Sunday the little lad died –

Broke mother dear.

And at last and for the least;

May mercy on us,

Nor thine or mine earth, best

To live in; with little fuss.

***

The poet worries on the calamities of nature and the tolerating human beings, either by rain or by sun. He wails … *'…can he hope for a relief ever'*. I wrote it when I faced the first drought in my life.

"Emergency Is A State Of Mind Not Country...., And Love Is The Base Of Human Life, Not Country."

My Unknighted Father

Navigate in the loch of goodly life,
Waif not Godfather natty, with rustic patches;
Nebular bemuse, his heart loggy at the cliff,
People nefarious, a "*neophyte*" he, heist all riches!
Like blooms b'dden heavenly incense,
Unacknowledg'd, 'benison the air and bride's neck'!
Evil not his heart, a foulless 'unread poesy' intense:
Stake mean, scriptures hoary on 'Ozhimandias' rock!
Sons pamper'd like me: bard lack'd sense;
Whom the 'heir - looms', copious thoughts like Pampa?
'Marquess not knight'd he in the masquerade dense;
'Naivette the candle' until lit, he plumb a.
Travell'd he in "*islands*"; bead'd hymns of sadness;
"If a rest would thou seek, Pa be our goodness."

***

As you can see the main character of the sonnet is my father, whole failure in life is due to his honesty and inability to make people know what he wants. See the term "unread poesy". I lament on his failures, acknowledging his abilities unused. [He had been a victim of his worst early setbacks of life] But he neither allowed me to take him out of the troubles he was surrounded by nor he was willing to accept my suggestions.

"If the death makes a poet legend, he lived in poverty."

Nature is the finest artist

Prophet And Prejudice

The domain of love may own,
Constellation countless; stars and moon,
The domain of heart mine may own,
Love more glare than stars very soon!
Bequeath'd my life and love,
A heart with hillside snow and flow;
Thou be in the domain of my love,
Sublime my psyche with a lot glow.

Said someone and someone aired,
Poets wrote, artistes died in mystique –
But, miraculous heaven of thoughts flay'd,
The wise lover; all for 'one and none' genetic,
This unmatch'd inheritance: virtue nil,
Idiots may find 'tug' the idiom till,
he final scream shall not have open'd-
'Her eyes', but may laugh and teas' belov'd!

In the life before or after pall-life,
"See no cloud, no bows; skies may wail,
The dead baby's mother's udders suffocate to feed!"
Mother cries, alas! Without tears: somebody's wife,
Went her child into lasting nap, blows whirling gale;
Faint her face so the nature around, need –
Someone and something to peel-off –
Indifferent melancholy; with aesthetic goof.

Pinion strokes that seek airy wind,
Triumvirate of thee, me and all shalt reprimand,
Trivial feel times under the trivet of gnawing thoughts,
Close to my eyes those *pinion strokes* clots,
Deepest as in darkling mid-sea bottom;
Pearls, mollusc windless den there so dim,
Clasping luminous venom and savage whales too,
I'm in beginning passion doused, solely we two.

Palpitating heart mine may be brought,
Tautology of rubbish speech: no melody that-
Ever before; finishing autumn, season fifth –
Impart me with –spoonful poison and milk,

Either one nourish; neither another, perish;
Hardrock alternative; aberration of heartless death.
But no gore; bloodless massacre, sparse love bulk,
"All poets may be born by beloveds such, *hardly cherish*"!

Swore the princess before the Cross blind with tears,
For the span left to walk with; glowing eve around,
Ignore the scent of bloom'd jasmin's b'neath mid-sun,
When the crowd tied up night late; beetle flies,
Mortal both; palliate my b'loved now having bound,
Tease nor ease me, yet wish'd my season –
Of sensual planks to be nor more on board ,
Leave the *sea soon*, fly like seabirds without guard.

Stooping my nerves, half-way honourless exodus;
None shalt be comrade yours, better least plead,
You shalt be well posted amidst 'modus'-
Modest conceal veracity, pretend and fled;
This is life! This is mortality of immortal trust!
"Five count fingers fine on palm thine,
May you count which lucre good on merit line?"

The shoddy timber merchn't lov'd maid –
Who serv'd cuisine wooden: easy to be fir'd,

Met nooks and hedges' shades with hir'd dreams,
Succinct looks, kiss'd, n'ver I witness'd;
Hook'd in the anchor clasps, n'ver return'd!
Her lover merchant; lusty, penny eyed dreams,
Hir'd well benefitted herself: queen from cuisine;
"Admire your Queen: bloody poets write lyrics of sin!"

Fail a b'loved today: unboutonnier'd my attire exterior,
Effervescence the reek of algay'd memories past,
The dreadful belfry bang: unfenc'd the rival warrior,
Sporadic fear my heart fills, unsold memories burst,
"Where shall I go, on to grave or to be brave?
The fear'd ferry moves, oars sunk deep, and keep-
Its spook afloat, but afraid without wave!"
Many more brooks I see under valley steep.

The morning mist, Iwalk, sheds moments lovely,
Warning my way forth zooming band of beetles',
Seldom takes aback to sack feelings hurt lonely;
Sheath of cold rinse my nose; feel as if toothless;
The domain of love may own,

Constellation countless; stars and moon,

The being rest mine may be alone;

Shalt, shalt n'ver mourn; unless a thunder morn'!

***

Lovelorn poet, a bit shattered and at the same time remembering the good and bad times of the past. He presumes whether his beloved of dreams could be true or a shame as he mentions, he is unwilling to commit or to continue "...lusty, penny eyed dreams ...". This clearly expresses that he loses his faith on anyone and he is afraid to go ahead with anyone.

"Light makes you see the invisible, love is the light in darkness."

Fuhrer Corpse

I had a canine so rogue and dark,
Royce his looks, smart and bark;
Frawn at the one who tresses his border,
Alert and brawn my beast, I boast louder.

Roving his eyes in black mount nights,
As if scanning beams of miners; no dull his sights,
Gnawing his fluid tongue every now and then –
Dare I may, kiddish not he, fool him my brethren.

He was more a Hitler, but gentle and crest \,
Bound his days in wooden shed so short,
Scared every stray with his royal roar best,
Round his nights my home around armour grit.

Wakes he wee morns, may provoke my sleep,
All he set-in for a day sleep after breakfast,

Dislik'd he bath and fly –less day and weep,
He being chain'd till night so dark and folks rest.

Twirl his sickle ponny back; loyal tail,
May be remember'd his unmatch'd 'shake hands',
He was nam'd Dicky, better than derrick's tale,
Well featur'd his bones and brought up in our hands.

Served us and severed after years five,
Derived him love, loyalty and vigour in life;
Beast it, and tamed his brave bones to strive,
His royal black and murmured licks all to grief.

Fed nothing his days last, bred in water,
Distant to food, loathful to serve as he tired;
My darling brethren; *I hate to see him later!*
Visible his bones and less sharp teeth, I silently cried.

Stable he more to grave, rare he stands;
Unable the physique and words ours to cure, remain –
"Oh, my dear friend", left he in pain stings,
Forgive me thy master,"batted eyes in loathsome pain" .

Disloyal indeed, I chatter in depair,

Conscience takes me into the sorrow unrepair';

Soulless the creature he: makes master's soul cry,

"Soul be the instinct from God to his dogs, not yet we cry!

He lay no royal, cried loyally us neither in return-

His majestic rows of mane set close calm and no frawn;

"End more a prince be flowered, sceptor remains,

Never more condole, when hands drop the sword and fines!"

My dog too died in agony and at tender,

His unerroenous jumps and murmur render;

The tales of uncared grave and marshy mud-

Spaded down to his rough cool body *without guard*!

***

Skuddy my lad shabby at home,

Jealous his neighbours shook his belt in pride;

Mannish he was, but brutal the hoodlums,

Plotted to finish him, my brethren dear lad!

No mean dog was he, dined in venison and fried pie;
Last long his dinner no more than minute one!
Pass time in loose mud and unkempt, morn' every by,
Reach in "inane and shy'' and love by then looks "tired none"!

Breed his hound, bred in bound;
Spared never his foes in lounge else found,
He barked as if horned Royce's rough and loud;
Trigger the fright in bait every, soon be shroud.

Heart that may be ripped, once solicited,
Per-contra let not live in recital fair;
Onus being loved, bonus in limpid pain cited,
Bestowed to be remembered; while left in despair.

Ramp he brisk, ram he brought,
Roam never any, stayed apart the unwanted;
Rapacious he in being fed a lot beef and sought,
More in course three, ever he granted!

He had his crass and caressed in wild love,

Tamed many, but rained in discreet my lad;

Neither brothers more in being, yet me in steamed blow,

Ever thy master be in the "*ferry undrowned*", so sad!

***

It is an easy and straight poem, remembering my most loved pet during my high school days. As an animal lover, I never kept my pet Dicky away from my life. He (not it) was loved by everyone in the family. I remember the way we played each other, enjoyed his manners …! He is visible like a black pearl in my eyes. He died of intestinal ulcer and his last days were tearful.

"Which is the most beautiful living thing in the world? It's your foolishness to find the answer"

The Host Of West Land

Forth thy mother sweet, ‘off-home’ sons;
Snuggle the unsniff’d music unheard in hearts-
Sergeant soignee, fought till moon grins!
Broke the ‘armada’! Sweat the ‘soul’ fell against ‘forts’!
Arid the ‘westland’ shanties in hostile sand;
Barbecued ‘em in morphined meat,
O’er the sherried wine, the swined brigand;
Maelstorm’d regions ‘em: patridges’ treat!
‘Soggy’ may the decamped plane and sojourned-
Blooded both: flagged high on mothers’ crest;
‘Nor citadel or a clean way – let found –
Sound for mothers, West and East, propped best!
“Let thee cuff be pieced, mine limbs free,
Dismantle façade, with the blind sword’s spree!

***

The poet wants to know why the two countries (India and Pakistan) are arch rivals for over seven decades. These countries have conflicts till now, both don’t want to realize the errors committed by each other. In the sonnet I wanted convey that ‘hatred cannot bring love’, therefore stop blaming each other and find a resolve.

Nature's craft, love at first sight

"A Sage Is Fit For This World But Not When You Are Alive."

The Final Hour Kiss

I

Lit someone pyre for the dusk,
Mid-June fervent environ seem'd,
Anger'd sun sung quartette without mask,
With all coft, far me from furnac'd –
Smith's camera; idle and slept;
"Went all pilgrims in illusion'd brain,
Like mouthpieces reach its all height.
I felt, Beethoven sung pure train –
Of melodic memoirs, hand'd thousands –
Sprint'd like hydral creatures."
Downcast tendrils stood sweat'd,
In the pall'd green, rye and mustard;
Gloom,gloom the sad dusk; brides crie'd –
With all my love's words I said,
Eas'd , fond and slowly I drawn'd .
Pass'd fractions like brisk'd ostrich,
'Brave'd nil all actions: Psyche blown'd,

Well; seen counties in misty smooch!'
"There a flame! No heat, a halo very slow,
Shroud'd in Godly white, a neat jasmine petal,
Long till toes unseen; with golden glow,
Star –headed sceptor, rightward hold, not fatal."
I deem'd, afright enough; well-wrought crown,
Fitt'd like God and sooth; half fell,
Left hand hold flower'd kettle close to gown.
No dream! No shout, fear'd will;
Matured the psyche about to scream;
Ear'd a heavenly apparition,'she spoke':
"Wake up,my son .....wake up to own my realm,
Bride thine, my child Lucica all in a hook!"
Selfly grab'd mighty – a heavy sword;
As if smith beaten fresh and a shield,
Both I own'd :Helen of Troy I remember'd ,
Benison'd hands mine: Molten irons,
Banish'd the spirit in unseen speed,
'Cited me with dew odouring Rose, full blown.'

II

Erect me with chutzpa, psyche's d'sire,
Resurrect the passion condemn'd past:
Withal the wintry eves: Lucica's leisure,
In the plane-tree shade hold with all zest;
Roosting the naughty chicks flew past,
Gentle was the peeping –wind; loosen'd
Clasp'd arms, lovely plums, I'm lost!
Un-pre-deem'd kisses and scann'd,
Craz'd fingers in my fluent hair,
"Oh!My love, Lucica: tidal coast –
Of my heart roar'd; I lov'd …my heir,"
Nips all fear, led the cupid so fast.

III

Tett'd my pony, rode all the terrain,
As if wing'd; through dales and towers;
Valliant a lover, when wails Valentine,
Rain'd the sky; token'd triumph lover's!
Musty dead meadow, on night seventh,
Perch'd still on saddle, the brawn ponny's
Watch'd the hill, cudd'd the 'hey-month',
Nags crickets and mantis, night's symphonies.

Leaden the greasy thicket, I sate nor –
I mayn't; I lay, embrace'd eyelids;
'Fluke! Deafening apparition I hear:
"Wake up my son Antonyo …"! She leads,
"Thee?" Me in aghast and obey'd.
No musette, no munchies, no munition;
Mural musics! Skies stood afled.
So nigh my love's prison, I in ignition;
Honouring morn sun ray, I saw in moan;
Having all I reach'd, soon 'halo left'.
B'mused, *nud'd* the Mighty God's boon,
Assur'd the armour'd metal hid, and drift –
Mule fac'd troops, with gunt and grimace,
Seeme'd dopey creatures dormant and vice!

IV

The cause in the course of being,
Until death deg by deg I love Lucica,
Foster child of unchristen'd spirit: Godly thing;
Doomsday ultimate? Like stoic silica,
Faze with all force, silent dome:
Dole –ful my heart, "where am I for?"

Fettle my love in undriven shore.
'Dire', dare not my svelte fiancée,
May whole my "unfeline heart's storm"
"Fey!" Oft echoes; "What seems fecund fiance?"

V

'Belated Shabbat' lays I did in 'chaste',
Rac'd the mauve clouds with purpose;
Meckintosh pull'd I down damp and post
Me against Alaska hills, Like valor'd heroes;
Fill'd the goblets of mind with sad wine;
Like a pree-mie expects gentle caress-
Maverick lover: Dire strife yet to begin!
Do lovers strife all ever with quite compress?
Why do all in quirk, my arteries?
Sedan I search'd, a hand I sought.
"Immoral to the shelv'd characteries,
Writ nails, off dat'd vellums ever may hurt!"
Comforting bosom: Soldier's fairy land;
"Ethic the lov'd so proud; when he brav'd,
Shakespeare indited epic of Utopian brand."
Oh! My love Lucica, all to end the shrewd,
Destin'd tryst with evils, mighty my bod;

Horn'd my heart for the "apparition'd mission"!
"Strife, my son Antonyo, for thine love,
Hard, hard, you God's nominee- YOU BLESS'D."
With thunder borne sky and golden arrow,
I vow'd! I heard the motherly spirit pass'd.

VI

Eighth day, distant my home: For the game!
The cannibals I saw, warpaint'd and threw –
Tridents like 'horizontal –rain', all came
Untouch'd, I fell'd in brisk and the horse drew –
Rear and vanish'd; I dared and ahead,
In the noon-tide battle, rotated me –
In aweful abrupt, hissed my sword,
Like Saturn's halo! Nose div'd into the homey
Hell one by one! With nut-some march,
Bloodi'd knife: The dusk'd evils',
Deft and strategic I pac'd, west pole seems notch,
The tiring sun like peels oranges',
"Oh, thee saturnine sun, hear my yell,
My nacre belov'd, all Godly things I need."
When the pekes eat pemmican in saloons of knell,

‘Sibilant of all the satyr breed of domain,
Nosey the obloquy demons in the reign;
‘My love Lucica, shed blood stain’d tears’,
Like a shyster’s victim in ‘senseless box’!
On the veld of num-skull’d mules,
Broad falchions broken in the ‘bleedy influx’!
Umbra hid the prism –topp’d witches’ forts.
Cruis’d battalion like stallion not saned;
Dread’d figures, brut unwrits,
Crush’d all the shrapnel: subjects clon’d;
With riches of all witches, hatches to fetch,
Unscrupulous, rude butchers to lamp,
Warheads, ‘lacked heads’, to unmeter’d stretch!
“Smirch unfit to live all grieve lump,
Even my Earth, life without life, Oh! God.”
With quite might, benison’d when left,
I master’d unlearned skills, blaster’d in all fad,
“Venus” I’ve seen adoring with gold and opt –
To a verdical non-troppo, masterly sung,
Scoop’d in unseen prowess, I blatantly charg’d;
Strokes of tinkl’d fire, no song but pang
Usher’d new ‘delight’ and I barg’d.

Bate little, my pander'd wounds,

Stood with full hood, pejorative mountains –

Of lethal rebels, squall'd the thirsty hounds,

"Bleeding ordeal for love, of love by saints!"

VII

Jerry built evils: unfuell'd locomotives

Jive their way, hire the blood for no job,

Perquisite till perish, so hail the motives!

Like pot –sherd the sky, I saw the nineth morn's rob.

"Hail thou apparition!" I saw the Castle,

Blasphemous domain! Prairie of fat-heads!

Soon the morn, flown in, sprain'd me fossil!"

Like gnats and helminths, throbbing to entire bloods,

On the dirty locus flood'd in blood …blood..red!

Feck nor I'm, still with python grip;

On the 'mighty' knife, prolong I not fed;

Endear'd my 'sick' for the puck's group!

VIII

'Quell' the shamble, I hope: Bled my bod;

Finish'd yet nor, droop my lungs in bid-

Confide on thou lap my darling 'glad',
Unrhythm'd spoors, no spears from any side,
I walk'd faster than a snail, tumble;
My limbs, nigh'd the blood stain'd threshold,
A cool wind hush'd, fondl'd my armour'd ankle –
To head, felt only in my blood soak'd cold –
Neck and face, oblig'd to my disease!
Shov'd slowly, dark unliv'd cab, in –
With plaguing pain, no sick-bed to seize!
"Laid I sure, rest in dream: I've seen.

IX

Wintry days of *joi-de-vi-vre*, with my love,
Clamm'd hands, soft and built, in all eve,
The doves flew, love birds sung,
Lewd river-end, mushroom'd forest,
Rainbow'd sky, cloud'd with frenzi'd swing,
Pubic your kisses, sweet cherubic lust;
Want'd hugs, end'd in shrugs without aghast,
"N'ver dies, n'ver dies the lov'd days,
Eager with all vigour like sandalwood nice"!
Obey'd passion, exchang'd in fashion;

Laz'd on your thighs:fine furred cushion,
Shown all the shores, rivers and ambits,
When enter'd in teen's rose garden –
"Brewsome in myrrh, when sued love invites,
Lieu all paltry, set to roost, breast broaden."
When cried the bells of St. Ann,
And decreed we with solemn will,
Sham'd you in the staggering crowd of Sun,
Like marble mannequin with gold foil.
Ecologues heard us, whilst travelogue –
Under the icing vales, were sincere like 'fog'-
Nubile sibling of St. Agnes' child, I pride.
"Faith whom love, and how one ever –
Sheath her arms in assuring stride;
Trust, trust and trust alone, be sure, and n'ver"!
Thine arms: my valour, thine love: my power;
The wander'd 'fairy lands', all my zeal,
Thou my word, thou my lead, thou my prayer,
"All the roses tender bring may I, shall
Set the bed tonight," oblivious snow breathe –
With your nursing nuzzle, Oh! What a world.

X

Woke like a spring, did where I?
Nubbin mission, unmet my love, stood and sight –
Joying few and a Demon, all well drunk on pie,
'Havoc the left riot', fit with *die-hard* twilight!
"Face the life –may rage, may bay, may hell,
May destin'd to be! As hearts fuell'd ambition,
Vers'd shall obfuscate, unobject: oaf I tell."
Rocky, marsh, terrain, plateau: in fusion,
Hard, weep, strife, endless sad,
Places to live in, forces to sieve in;
Phantasi'd my heart "no way to secede"!
Escort'd my sword: Mascot for my win!
"Licketi-split"! Obsess'd monsters shriek'd,
Encircl'd like granite rocks and hurray'd!
Sail the sun towards equator, slowly heats,
Hail none, like a sea mount, helpless; me,
"Strange! The sky rock'd with earth breaking stunts,"
All favoured'd, slogg'd, to the 'aw'd granite enemy
Skipp'd the seine, in obeisance I kiss'd,
The 'knife of just and might', blood dress'd!
Fillip in every cell, the foe-men puzzl'd,

Oddities pass'd each and won over the hold;
Hail-shower'd with b'friended tempest buzz'd,
Enter'd the Alcaza of alligators, where witches stroll'd;
No sentry unkill'd, I sure, smelt indoors-
Incens'd I n'ver! Signal to affray with all force!
'There!' the ogre I found in wild panic,
"Might of Satan very light' ere the sight of god,"
Curs'd in roughest, utmost pitch; hid I lack-
Any 'indoor eye', next to the rock gods fraud.

XI

"To the forth, and fray my son Antonyo,
Lack no dare, dire still to you, dart…dart…dart!"
Like a sybyl, the soliloquy proffess'd anew,
Prissy and not meant the 'dart'…part!
May Lucica, it meant; where she pent?
"Allay, Oh god…., the ordeal in lament,"
My finch, to revel the Mardi-Gras!
To hear the prothalamion, sung none, but me my lass,
'Oeuvre' thee in my every bit, my love,
Sad postulates of St. Ann, like octets of Elegy!
Hurtle all; "Wish ever, ever I lov'd no!"

The ‘Saturday’s tryst’ of human diology.
Gone too soon the ocular fantasy,
Inept nor a lover, to affray and confront;
Epics n’ver bloom’d in the full moon ecstasy:
Unless ‘swords’ and ‘fleets’ led to forefront!
Like a grandee in rank brav’d like Olympus,
Grant the “beloved’s” grand slam embrace:
“A reason to live, lesson to learn all the campus
Of love, lease of life with bride of grace.”

XII

Did I see, not the sun, until how much
Ward-west or rest? But the offing march,
Of time playing a sadist’s organ!
An eve of half-way riot, I deem,
Gist my heart in some sad slogan;
The eve we rest’d, without dreadful steam,
Not grant any thoughts of either Testaments:
The eve of Judas: the soul of breach attends,
The eve of ‘supper’: Penanc’d feast!
The eve of ‘His fulfilment’: Paradise lost!
Endorse too hard: ’This eve seems?’

Peeping the rays with masterly glimpse,
“Ne’er in faith, the unverily kids,
Of the shaming eve, like queans:
Unstaid lovelies with vases jargon’d sops.”
But;
The calm eve I eas’d with my love,
Shall say like a lute, or grapes mute;
Faithful awes eve, any ovation, any owe?
Orgulous why, the ale drunk stud!
Ordorous high for a loving lad; who said-
“Life is an idiot’s tale”, disloyal bard,
“Sweet, sweet the pies, don’t you erode,
Like lov’d one’s lips, even if bitter’d!”
On a golden raft I sail’d, sung all way,
‘She’ is my eve like Eve, so goodly,
Maroon’d some in the jolt of lasting hatred,
Shall n’ver said, blooms entire in fragrance,
Leaves all in green, hearts all bred-
In love, of the rhyme thee sought, may chance!
Lo! Vocalists’ olio; ‘mayn’t opium for the loner!’

"Not, grey any saga; no slay, no ploy,
If seas no whales; onus to the goner!"
Sooner or later espies the spirit of annoy.

XIII

Self-willed the demon, dine nor in lilt,
Fat fill'd horns torch'd, and a legman well built
Snoop'd ogre's ear, rose his brow like a bow,
"Light-out fear!" Largo my legs strict;
Like an unhurt cat to the bait, very slow;
Drew a shadow, unbreath'd me erect!
Went no more than my "shiv", unalarm he 'went'!
Hid I, through the leeward shades, but hint,
No leeway in the serri'd stouts!
No way than affray "leal to the sword!"
Lept in front, the frenzi'd louts.
Asunder'd skulls, aimlessly spread,
End-to-end I fought, limn I can't,
Like a lime moon grin'd.
The 'no-good' noggins fell'd, I saw
"Noh! innocuous, my will, through the show!"

XIV

The ogre, ugly fig' like a mug he bounc'd,
Shred my arm'd arm a bit, sped the knife
With a slang to the granite polish'd,
Sedulous moments in an octave,
Cumbersome predicament of 'phase',
In blinking haste head-butt'd me in all fatal
Sandwich'd to the near pillar and a 'ton daze'!
Curvet'd my heavi'd legs till he mortal!
Grab'd laid sword, no 'forces' to meet!
Fled the 'dastards' and abet,
The night-to-night fight: Vision'd fiasco.

XV

All ramp'd unseen, melt'd the fat,
Like an asylum for the butcher; but
"The aside, I heard were still more!"
Dumb the walls, pillars and bracing
Balmness of calmness, and shore-
None to the 'deck' of Lucica, air nicing,
The lethargic mirk, yet to reach Mardi-Gras!
In the vigil of love, I rode in all grades,
In dwaddle, twiddle; the tryst of b'muse:

"Tether where my bride?" My psyche pause!
"Revel!" A leaf fell'd like a 'mistake',
Another to another and to the next, all my sake!
Envoy'd the leaves, every pace I did,
End'd at last and dark cab, shut?
A turn of my head, no leaves spot!
An old piano sang in dreadful speed!
All a 'graveyard muteness: Oh! The leaves?
How view'd I in the dark: Castle oak'd,
Like 'glow-worms' enabl'd my 'bows'.
All left, no glow, no sight; like a blind,
Sped my sword in all air cling'd and struck-
To a wood on the wall and I inclin'd-
To the 'lit wall read': "Bad luck,
My son Antonyo; the cab of death this nam'd,
Die a maid, when in entry, so your lov'd!"
And an 'Angel song' conced'd in the rhyme,
Unsung by any; dank'd eyed hymn'!

XVI

For I stood, what art like Shake's sonnets!
Against the 'luminous art' on red like wood;
Glow'd until I read, 'flood my heart's' inlets,
Few moments of a trillion poesy, I read!
"All Greats", branch'd together,
With all princesses of Greek and Egypt,
Lure with all aloof, unending ballet!
"What-faultless-unfad'd-embrace wither,
All despair,-ever leisure-beautiful maids!"
Unchang'd the season, ever youth thy nights,
Dreams your fulfill'd and ever and ever,
Glorifi'd the lovers, ever like guards;
'Born you both, die you not lover,
No Lamia among; and no crowds.'

Boat-man journi'd with 'hands of hours',
Oppress'd hands in aghast and jess'd,
Buck'd in flumsy brain, a bard's horse!
Grate 'lots in brusque' and brush'd,
"A rhythmic brogue, broil'd in utter."
Bally with 'irrational wisdom'!

Buffet the buddies, bum and flutter,

Bullion the bard with ‘sterling kingdom’!

Chintzy the choleric ‘bucaneer’,

Sculling with the show of empowering mob,

Bodkin through his bodice and bole in cheer

When ‘husk’ the bestial without robe’,

I writ for the evils’ ‘ door panes’!

Tween benumb dark and ‘prolonging steam’!

My biathlon crusade versus predator insanes,

“Be-tim’d not, romanced in bibulous foam,

Bewailing love bisect’d heart,” blam’d she?

‘Blain my brain’, not even in the blitz-krieg,

“For ever I shalt: A matching dead sea!”

“Futures’ skies may be: A watching ice-berg!”

With all the exert, I sled the doz’d door!

Gasp’d my lungs, skim’d, like a sleuth did veer!

XVII

With a buffalo’s snore that clos’d,

Like a coal-mine, when world in nap,

I saw scant,owls even rumble, and nervous’d!

“Presto”! Apiec’d marble vase I found in the gap,

Of a second, singing angels, in *the Godly glow*!

Divine the full lit cab, all saw in mute;

A small throng of unasham'd furniture now,

Witness, "the slick lazing like a clarinet"!

Bled rose buds, unmov'd, lids shut –

Neat to be 'deep-wood-silence' like a freeze breeze-

Lucica lay unlike a mortem, but a cute-

'Sea- maid'in world's purest white: "Bridal fleece"!

Adieu'd every tear drop, arid my eyes;

Knelt me, sword I sheath'd, look'd blinkless;

A postlude I heard, wetting my eyes –

To an endless brooklet, streamlet and to the dankless,

Iced fingers of Lucica, kiss'd one!

Tear'd confessions; untriumph'd virtualities,

"Immortal the love: whose win it drawn,

Like dried blooms, for roaming beetles!"

Matters all for love: shatter all in the eve!

The eve of turbulence, that ever us grant'd!

The eve of Nazareth wept, all those gave,

"Similar rhym'd texts: all lovers lament'd!

B'trayals shalt accolade, for clever Lamia,

What shall for a fender'd lover, maim a?

XVIII

The mid-night ghosts cooed and phew'd,
Like a ridiculous mercinery, unalley'd my dread,
Arrayed my head in aching hooey
Ballet of witches, rough'd the horne!
The cancerous brain: Aimless milky way;
Lucica my life, my love, end: I now none!
"Strom'd the mounts, heavily rain'd;
Drop'd my brain, into a world so, so bright,
Dri'd the 'rose' in my chest 'petals' drain'd,
For the love'd Paradise, I fought end'd nought!"
Still sing the angels: no Elegy that was!
As if an eas'd sleep my love lay, "hard", she left!
"Sick all God, and soul died: alas!"
"Foul is foul and fair is fair", oft.
Bowl of ash'd olives is no 'fair' to bestow,
A nifty b'loved, supervising psyche, oh!
My almighty, amid marooning melancholy,
Amid empty coffins, I saw 'foul'd fair things'!
Honour to the grave: negate hearts visibly!
Lives b'reaved, unreliev'd: soully wings,
Pirouette the dreamy paranoid son the roads,
'Whence we once'; all that raids!

XIX

"How the texts know, whom will it be read?
How the words know, has who it 'written?"
How knows the mud, plough whom and sow'd?
How know the seasons, who-so-ever it smitten?
How the wind knows, how slow or verse blow?
Mint or melancholy, has it brought?
Not ever, meadows all green without water's flow,
Failed wail to the hailing sad flute.

XX

When sens'd a limpid silence, and I thought,
The illsens'd liaison of despair in drought,
Dens'd slow and slow to a deep plot:
No clash, no riot, but seen heat'd cloud,
Fell'd like ice-candies Lucica's hands, not
I wept, quietly reach'd for 'mooky sword';
Wood-winds not among the stupid society-
Of sung music: sorrow, sorrow but sorrow!
"Oh, benison'd St. Ann., I bated vicety,
To earn'd kingdom, I shalt follow!"
Throng'd all vices of vein-drought mongreals;
Bon'd debris, I saw "so fright" and in burials-

Of all fair thoughts, drew my knife,
Like a slut it 'borne' in my right arm:
"What a world of witch-heathen-and-grief!"
A ditch of huddling scorpions and a farm
Of hurt vipers, stilt walking witch gods!
Spar'd a "last offering", I bent to the "sleeping bride",
With 'weighing' heart in elevating nodes,
"Last, last the kiss for the lost, lost with abide."

XXI

Like a 'feckless tromp' I star'd,
'The marble face', seconds died, minutes born,
'Distanc'd in bran thin air', she smelt gourd-
Fresh fragrance! Lov'ly posh lawn;
"Unknown the season, the cocooning silence,
For ever, for all; ulti-mating romance;
Nor vision any, filthy the dales of death."
Post-date her psyche, with contouring faith,
Totter a heart from heaven high,she sees?
'Last the kiss I stamp'd, but a droplet
Embrac'd till nil, by the loyal eyes,'
"What leafless gardens for the engag'd pet!"

Slow was my paw for no show and glow,
For, all might that past in loathe breathe-
New light, like a lifer's last wit, when 'blow'
His heart in numerous 'hoofs' and 'bathe'-
Infront the proctor,and a mirror of ugly rite!

XXII

"Mardi-Gras",the Tue of hue: I in rue,
Lay a Hook of *His* taught stone, might
Ne'er least feast for the vices but my new
Lucica's psyche, all my merry; like a poser
I pragmatic will! Hectic the brute
Dagger, I wizz'd to my breast! Wonder!
In aghast I, plunder'd, vanish'd the stout
Sword, (shiv, knife and dagger),lieu shower'd,
Blooms of jasmine and daisy and I 'rock'd'!
"*A glee again*!" A cupid shined;
Grew the light and I heard with loud:
"Blesset, blesset the son.....,Antonyo, blesset thee,
Kiss thee Lucica, my child, for she ever with thee!"
With a brisk of lighting 'it' vanish'd;
Sped b'side my 'Love' I knelt and kiss'd:
"The tender warm like the spring of Eden morn,

Gestur'd she in the smock,as if were in fun!"
Hold her neatest, softest fingers to blinkless pose;
"Sure was the Apparition, sic was her shows"!
The fragrant oomph with half ope bed-dress,
'No air fill'd 'tween our hearts', and thus she part'd-
For moments, Lo! "Full adorn in gold and red!"
Unique match her tender lips so sweet.
So I in unseen white like a prince, stood-
We in sky or we in clouds or in water all great,
Every form, 'dried the bloomed petal and hand'd!'

XXIII

All eves nor portend with cripple gloom,
I saw, "what seen was fair, and not unfair!"
Triffle all curses when anguish bloom,
When mourn the lovelorn far or in fear?
N'ver see did her I? Look'd she marvel,
"Thank'd I my God with faith and might",
All the choirs of earth and heav', for the 'noel'
Today, "Lucica, my love: No tear tonight."
Pan-out the triumph so unbrav'd I,
All the very 'eve' under hastening sky;
"The slender belle, in perfectly pair'd,

Eyes and ears, arms and other norms,

As if a rose bouquet I palm'd,

The loveliest cheeks and sung the angels:

The herd b'fore: confluenc'd madrigal:

With no intervals, "without brain, boozing festival!"

Slovenly slid in 'all arm'd embrace and respite',

Lids clos'd my 'bride' and warm nostrils.

Tides of medley, 'those sung', heard, b'fit-

The ' *tam'd hills of love'*, hearken fiddles.

***

"*THE FINAL HOUR KISS*" is an unpretentious attempt to tell-a-tale of a brave lover and his beloved's ordeal on the backyard of an Epic carpet. The whole story revolves around a dream of hot summer day. Antonyo, who is braved by the Angels (God's messenger) for a gruesome battle with the demons who have made his love, Lucica, their captive. How far could you go to get your love. It is the fight between the 'good and the bad': love versus war! I recommend to read it in the same spirit, you might enjoy it.

I have followed the 'time and manner of language to match the period justice. If I failed in it, you may pardon me.

"Only love can solve problems in the world, however the silence of love is unaesthetically misunderstood by the human race."

poet

The Lover's Sigh

Dwadle the men fore and back, there stock the barren plane,

Feign or reign, he strolls on the sand or on the slush;

Meet few of the few, view of the new shores in the lane,

Make thee home of rocks or hopes, stride in the lush-

Of mansions- built of gore and lore, sigh I ever seek,

The tamarind, jasmine, cactus or lemony tales of the creek-

That twined with the gaily little streaks, a lover nay peak,

He sighs all the creeks, bays nothing, shades of the oak.

"The lover's sigh" the gales of benign bemuse shower-

Blooms of snow feathered lilies, garnered heart of gold.

Eager his mouth to sing the melody of sooth and hover

The halo of 'soulful harmony' in the doomed world.

"What thy home is built, pebbles or fables; rock or hope?"

Homed in both, yet a life long tales that mightn't suit-

The rhymes of a bard, hymns of philophile, I still cope

Quills never failed to quote the ballet of divine pursuit.

Spears and cleavers ripped the wailing hearts, dust and dire,

Robins, yet loved, moist sky and beneath the clouds,

"*Born the lions of love, saner, finer love bird, lair the buds,*

Love nays blind, but blends the bed of eternal bliss.

Nouveau ever it grows, never old, the heart beats endless.

From the mud to mount, oceans to oasis, pain to gain,

And, hate to love, the *sighed breeze may dance* the life,

Tenacious the love that heals the wounds or strain,

Audacious the lover who bleeds, silent relief,

Last the life, the soul of signs though sigh and height,

Love that coins and claim ingots shall strive in filth,

"That buds in the eve of care and bares in naught,

No lavish saffires, no manor, as love bids blithe."

For the mounts, the fields, the terrain, the creeks or sand,

The cannons, the gallops, the spears and the garrisons,

All that bloopers the emperor's court, lover's band-

On the shore of trust, sigh on the hearts' morison.

***

The poet thinks about the ways a true lover relieves himself from the strife and wars of people. Love can be found in every corner of the world; either in a war field or a farmer's field. There are people who consider money with diamond and wealth, but the poets laughs at those who do not understand the essence of love because 'love emerges not from money, but it is the clean air between two hearts'. It can solve problems.

Poetic Conclusion

Why do people write poetry? Why can't they write an essay or book? These questions can be answered as follows- do you think music is important in life? Can't the people speak those sentences and drum around? Poetry is essentially the result of a beautiful dimension of thoughts and rhythmic language. It is essentially the 'beautification of language in its sublime form'. Poetry is the most beautiful form of linguistic creativity. And, language is the response to a an emotional outflow. Poetry is, thus, the silent music of language. If poetry and music are blended together, it would create a surreal magic of symphony and euphoria. The lyrics written for a song is essentially a piece of poetry. Can we think about the world without 'music'? It is nothing, but heaven without God. The first form of human description on anything could have been in the form of poetry.

Indeed, it is an era of 'foolish poetry and linguistic abuse', and that create an impediment in the emerging poets around the world. We cannot find a John Milton or Shakespeare today. One could not find a John Keats anywhere in the human history in the past 300 years! Come forward, let us make this world a beautiful place not only for us, but also for the future generations.

Poetry is love, and one cannot love anyone without poetry.

Poet

www.ingramcontent.com/pod-product-compliance
Lightning Source LLC
LaVergne TN
LVHW041610070526
838199LV00052B/3082
* 9 7 8 9 3 6 5 5 4 5 5 6 2 *